W9-APX-643

# BASKETBALL

## BY DREW SILVERMAN

CONTENT CONSULTANT
SABRINA SCOTT
PROFESSIONAL BASKETBALL PLAYER

Printed in the United States of America,
North Mankato, Minnesota
102011
012012

 THIS BOOK CONTAINS AT LEAST 10% RECYCLED MATERIALS.

Editor: Chrös McDougall
Copy Editor: Anna Comstock
Design and Production: Craig Hinton

**Photo Credits:** Jacquelyn Martin/AP Images, cover (bottom); iStockphoto, cover (top); John Swart/
AP Images, 1; Susan Ragan/AP Images, 5, 11, 59 (middle); John Gaps III/AP Images, 7; Lon Keller/
Library of Congress, 13, 58 (top); Francis Benjamin Johnston/Library of Congress, 19, 58 (middle);
AP Images, 21, 29, 31, 35, 58 (bottom), 59 (top); Charles Knoblock/AP Images, 27; Michael O'Brien/
AP Images, 37; Andrew D. Bernstein/NBAE/Getty Images, 39; Douglas C. Pizac/AP Images, 43, 59
(bottom); Eric Draper/AP Images, 47; Mark J. Terrill/AP Images, 49; Ed Betz/AP Images, 53; Jamie
Schwaberow/NCAA Photos/AP Images, 54; Mike Ehrmann/AP Images, 57

**Library of Congress Cataloging-in-Publication Data**
Silverman, Drew, 1982-
  Basketball / by Drew Silverman.
    p. cm. -- (Best sport ever)
  Includes index.
  ISBN 978-1-61783-141-6
  1. Basketball--Juvenile literature. I. Title.
  GV885.1.S45 2012
  796.323--dc23
                          2011033782

# CHAPTER 1

# THE DREAM TEAM

The question was never if the Dream Team would win. Nor was it by how many points it would win. The question with the Dream Team was whether this was the greatest team in sports—in the *history of sports,* that is.

Men's basketball had been added to the Olympic Games in 1936. Until 1992, however, the United States had always sent amateur players rather than the top professional players from the National Basketball Association (NBA). But all of that changed in 1992. After the amateur US squads began to struggle against opposing teams that had professional players, the US national team opened up to NBA players. The team of NBA superstars who went to the Olympics in Barcelona, Spain, representing the United States became known as the Dream Team.

The Dream Team's Michael Jordan sails high above teammate Magic Johnson to block a shot against Croatia during the 1992 Olympic Games.

The US team featured 12 of the nation's basketball icons. Three of the players—Michael Jordan, Earvin "Magic" Johnson, and Larry Bird—would eventually retire as three of the greatest players in basketball history. As of 2011, 11 of the 12 players had been inducted into the Naismith Memorial Basketball Hall of Fame. That list included centers Patrick Ewing and David Robinson and forwards Karl Malone and Charles Barkley. Only Christian Laettner, the lone college player on the squad, had not been enshrined.

Even the Dream Team's head coach was a star. Chuck Daly had led the Detroit Pistons to NBA championships in 1989 and 1990. But even he had never seen anything quite like this.

"It was like Elvis and the Beatles put together," Daly said. "Traveling with the Dream Team was like traveling with 12 rock stars. That's all I can compare it to."

## STATISTICAL LEADERS

Charles Barkley, a forward for the Phoenix Suns, was the leading scorer on the Dream Team. He averaged 18 points per game and made more than 70 percent of his shots. Michael Jordan was second at 14.9 points per game, while Karl Malone was third at 13 points per game. Malone and Patrick Ewing tied for the team lead with 5.3 rebounds per game. Scottie Pippen averaged a team-high 5.9 assists.

Dream Team stars Magic Johnson, *left*, and Michael Jordan exchange high fives during their 116–48 win over Angola at the 1992 Olympic Games.

## Pure Dominance

The gold medal was never in doubt. The Dream Team won its eight Olympic games in Barcelona by an average of 43.8 points. The closest game came in the gold-medal contest. That was a 32-point win over Croatia, 117–85.

The Dream Team was not just a dominant basketball team, though. It was a team filled with iconic athletes who dazzled the global audience with their exciting performances. Throughout the tournament, the US players threw down jaw-dropping dunks and shot from places on the court of which most basketball players could only dream. In the process, they set basically every Olympic basketball record that existed. As Dream Team point guard John Stockton said, "It was basketball on a different level."

## Constant Attention

Basketball was already one of the most popular sports in the United States. Millions of fans watched college and NBA games on TV and in arenas. And Jordan, Bird, and Johnson were household names. The excitement of having those superstars all together on one team drew up plenty of excitement back home. The global audience waiting in Barcelona and watching on TVs around the world was pretty excited too.

The Dream Team was so popular that the players received many bizarre requests from their opponents. For example, in the middle of one game, an opponent was seen waving at the bench. One of his teammates was taking a picture of him guarding

### A NEW HOBBY

Years after the 1992 Olympics, French journalist Olivier Pheulpin attempted to explain why France had so much basketball talent: "What happened is easy to explain," he said. "After the Dream Team in 1992, many of our best athletes began playing basketball instead of soccer. Simple as that."

Johnson—during the action. And another opponent asked Johnson for his jersey—before the game even started.

Their immense popularity also had its downfalls. Due to safety concerns, the Dream Team decided to stay in a hotel away from the Olympic Village. For protection, police officers constantly surrounded the players. But even the police officers wanted autographs from the US superstars.

## World Growth

Basketball was slowly growing around the world before the Dream Team took over the 1992 Olympic Games. Afterward, the sport's popularity exploded. During the 1991–92 NBA season, there were fewer than 20 international players in the NBA. At the start of the 2000–01 season, that number had grown to 45 foreign players from 28 different countries. And at the start of the 2010–11 season, there were a record 84 international players from 38 countries in the NBA.

Among those 84 players were several superstars. Tim Duncan, a power forward from the Virgin Islands, led the San Antonio Spurs to four NBA championships in his first 11 seasons. Three of those titles came alongside point guard Tony Parker from France and shooting guard Manu Ginobili from

Argentina. Dallas Mavericks forward Dirk Nowitzki (Germany), Los Angeles Lakers forward Pau Gasol (Spain), and Phoenix Suns guard Steve Nash (Canada) were All-Stars, as well.

Yao Ming, a 7-foot-6 center from China, was the first pick in the 2002 NBA Draft. Yao was voted to start at the All-Star Game in each of his first seven NBA seasons with the Houston Rockets. Yao had first developed a love of basketball by watching Ewing on television from China. Parker, meanwhile, was watching Jordan on TV in France when he decided, "I'm going to play in the NBA someday."

As more international players began starring in the NBA, international competition between national teams improved as well. Even though Team USA featured top NBA players, it only won a bronze medal at the 2004 Olympic Games. Behind Ginobili, Argentina beat Italy for the gold medal. Spain

## WORLD CHAMPIONS

The World Championship is the biggest tournament among basketball national teams outside of the Olympic Games. It takes place every four years. Team USA began sending NBA players to that tournament following the 1992 Olympic Games. After winning the 1994 World Championship, Team USA did not win it again until 2010. It only finished sixth at the 2002 tournament. The team took bronze medals in 1998 and 2006. However, the US squad won the title at both the 2008 Olympic Games and the 2010 World Championship. The World Championship for Women began in 1953, three years after the first men's tournament.

*From left:* Scottie Pippen, Michael Jordan, and Clyde Drexler pose with their gold medals after winning the 1992 Olympic Games.

also emerged as a powerful basketball nation. It won the 2006 World Championship, which is the second biggest international basketball competition. Spain followed that up with a silver medal at the 2008 Games.

International fans fell in love with the Dream Team. It was not just the players' skills, but also the way they played together and had fun on the court that captivated fans. The US players were global superstars. Players all over the world wanted to be just like them.

"I don't think you'll see another team quite like this," Daly said before he passed away in 2009. "This was a majestic team."

# THE BEGINNINGS

Basketball is a high-flying game. The best players can run fast, jump high, and slam dunk with ease. In 1891, however, basketball looked nothing like that.

At first, basketball was a slow, simple game. It had nine players on each side. The ball was a soccer ball. The baskets were peach baskets hung from gymnasium railings. And after each made basket, someone had to climb up a ladder to retrieve the ball. The sport has come a long way since Dr. James Naismith invented it in the late 1800s.

## What's Up, Doc?

Naismith was a physical education instructor from Ontario, Canada. In 1891, he was working at a Young Men's Christian

Dr. James Naismith invented basketball while teaching physical education at a YMCA in Springfield, Massachusetts.

## IT'S A START

In 1906, nets began to replace peach baskets as the goals for basketball. And by 1929, basketball finally resembled the sport we know today. Basketball courts had iron rims and nets, and the court dimensions were generally the same throughout the country.

Association (YMCA) in Springfield, Massachusetts. His boss, Dr. Luther Gulick, had a problem. He wanted to attract athletes to the YMCA when baseball and football were not in season. But he did not know how.

"Doctor, we can invent a new game that will meet your needs," said Naismith, who was 29 years old at the time.

Naismith knew the sport would have to involve a ball, just like the popular baseball and football. And he also wanted it to have some kind of goal, like in soccer and lacrosse. But he did not want the defensive players to crowd around it. So, he decided to put the goal above their heads.

Once the basic guidelines were in place, Naismith introduced the sport to his class on December 21, 1891. Some people suggested the sport be named "Naismith ball." However, he decided to instead call it "basket ball." Over the years, it became known as basketball.

The sport received positive reviews from players and observers. When the YMCA athletes went home for Christmas that year, many introduced the sport to their hometowns. And just like that, the sport of basketball was born.

## Branching Out

In January 1892, the first official rules of basketball were published. The guidelines appeared in *The Triangle*. That was the school newspaper for Springfield College in Massachusetts. Naismith originally had 13 rules. Some of them are still in effect today, such as "the ball may be thrown in any direction with one or both hands" and "a player cannot run with the ball."

Around the same time, basketball games began to appear in Massachusetts, New Jersey, New York, and Pennsylvania. Games

**EASILY AFFORDABLE**

There is one main advantage that basketball has always had over other sports such as football, baseball, and hockey. It is the fact that all you need to play basketball is, by definition, a basket and a ball. Even back in the early 1900s, a basketball only cost a couple of dollars. These days, it is still much cheaper to buy a basketball than it is to purchase a baseball bat or a hockey stick. And basketball requires no additional equipment, such as football pads, hockey skates, or a baseball glove.

As a result, many successful basketball players are men and women that have come from poor beginnings. Basketball is an activity that inner-city children can turn to in order to find entertainment, exercise, and, in some cases, extreme wealth.

were being played both indoors and outdoors. However, teams did not always agree on the rules. Teams known as barnstormers traveled around the country. They played whatever opponents they could find, regardless of the rules. The most successful barnstorming team was the New York Original Celtics.

## Initial Problems

Basketball was a fairly dangerous sport at first. Games were very physical. It was not uncommon for players to bleed or get badly injured during games. Since the rules were not clearly defined, the referees struggled to control the games.

It was also tough to control the fans. Spectators began to interfere with the games. To control them, many YMCAs built steel cages around the outside of the courts. However, players began to throw opponents into the cages during games. As a result, basketball

### OLYMPIC DREAMS

Men's basketball was added to the 1936 Olympic Games in Berlin, Germany. On April 7, 1936, Dr. James Naismith was invited to toss the ceremonial ball for the first Olympic basketball game. Naismith often said that this was the highlight of his life. The United States won the first Olympic gold medal in basketball that year. The US team defeated Canada in the gold-medal game 19–8. Team USA actually won the first seven gold medals in men's basketball before losing to the Soviet Union in 1972. Women's basketball was not introduced into the Olympic Games until 1976.

players became known as "cagers." The nickname stuck for many years.

In addition, some people became concerned that basketball was becoming *too* popular. They felt that basketball was just a game—not real exercise. And it was drawing people away from traditional athletic activities, such as gymnastics and body-building.

## College Beginnings

The first basketball game between two colleges took place on February 9, 1895. The Minnesota School of Agriculture defeated Hamline University 9–3, which was a typical score at the time. The game was played on a handball court in the basement of the Hamline science building. There were nine players on each side.

The game continued to expand. In April 1905, representatives from 15 colleges met in Philadelphia, Pennsylvania. Together, they created the Basket Ball Rules Committee. Then in 1909, the Intercollegiate Athletic Association of the United States took in the committee. One year after that, in 1910, it was renamed the National Collegiate Athletic Association (NCAA). The NCAA is still organizing college sports today.

## Women Get Their Turn

Many people did not believe women should participate in strenuous activities at the time. Senda Berenson was the director of physical education at Smith College in Massachusetts. She heard about Naismith's game and wanted to create a similar game that was appropriate for women. In 1899, she published the "Official Rules" of women's basketball.

The original women's rules gave each player a designated area where she had to stay. Women were not allowed to steal the ball from each other. And no woman was allowed to dribble more than three times.

Just like the men, women quickly fell in love with basketball. They enjoyed the athletic freedom, as well as the competition. The sport gave women a sense of

### BABE DIDRIKSON

Many people consider Babe Didrikson to be the greatest female athlete of all time. The Texas native was an Olympic track-and-field star as well as a professional golfer. She also was one of the first women's basketball stars.

In high school, Didrikson was an All-American basketball player in 1930, 1931, and 1932. During that time, she was playing for a team called the Golden Cyclones. In 1931, she led the Cyclones to the national championship. Two years later, she started a team called Babe Didrikson's All-Americans. The team traveled the country playing against men's teams. Didrikson was usually the best player on the court—male or female.

"Before I was in my teens, I knew exactly what I wanted to be," Didrikson once said. "I wanted to be the best athlete who ever lived."

Girls from Western High School in Washington DC play basketball around 1899.

confidence and control that they generally did not have at home. Still, some people worried about the amount of physical activity. Critics were especially concerned because many women's teams actually played by men's rules. Physical education expert Dudley Sargent wrote an article called "Are Athletics Making Girls Masculine?" Others wondered if playing basketball endangered women's ability to reproduce. And there was concern that the sport was causing women to become selfish.

Ultimately, though, the opposite became obvious. Basketball was helping men and women stay healthy. It also was showing the importance of teamwork.

# CHAPTER 3

# THE PROFESSIONAL PERSPECTIVE

The first professional basketball game was on November 7, 1896. The Trenton Basketball Team from New Jersey defeated the Brooklyn YMCA from New York. Trenton players received $15 each for their work.

Two years later, in 1898, the first professional basketball league was developed. The National Basketball League (NBL) included six teams. All of the teams were located in Pennsylvania or New Jersey. The league lasted five seasons before folding due to lack of interest.

A few regional leagues came and went in the following years. In 1925, the American Basketball League (ABL) was created with the hopes of forming a nationwide league. The ABL

Nat Holman was one of the first professional basketball stars while playing for the Original Celtics and other barnstorming teams in the early 1900s.

**SEEING RED**

There was no true women's professional league during the 1940s and 1950s. But there were still competitive games around the country. A women's team known as the All-American Red Heads began touring the nation in 1936. The women played against men's teams in a fancy style similar to the Harlem Globetrotters. Some of the players were actual redheads. The ones who weren't either wore wigs or dyed their hair. The Red Heads regularly played more than 200 games a year before they folded in 1986.

stretched from Boston, Massachusetts, to Chicago, Illinois. It was successful for more than five years. However, it ran into financial problems in the early 1930s and had to fold.

The Midwestern Basketball Conference (MBC) was the next major league. It was formed in 1935. Local factories supported many of its teams financially. By 1938, the MBC changed its name to the NBL. It was the fifth different league to go by that same name.

In 1946, the Basketball Association of America (BAA) was created as well. Hockey team owners looking to fill their arenas when their teams were out of town formed the league. On August 3, 1949, the BAA and the NBL merged. The end result was the NBA.

## A League of Their Own

The NBA began with 17 teams in the 1949–50 season. Some teams were from major cities. Among them were the New York Knickerbockers and the Boston Celtics. Others were from small cities such as the Anderson Packers from Indiana and the Sheboygan Red Skins from Wisconsin.

Following its first season, the NBA slimmed down to 11 teams. The league was not nearly as popular as it is today. That made it hard for teams to make enough money to survive. By 1954–55, the league was down to eight teams. It would remain at that number until the 1961–62 season.

With so few teams, it was easy for one team to dominate the league. In the NBA's early years, that team was the Minneapolis Lakers. The Lakers won the final BAA championship in 1948–49. Then they won four of the first five NBA titles.

### CAMPUS LIFE

College basketball began to thrive during World War II, from 1939–1945. During this time, some college players were too young or too tall to be drafted into the military. Others were allowed to complete their military training on campus. As a result, college basketball began to grow in popularity during the 1940s and 1950s. The first men's NCAA Tournament, a postseason format to determine a collegiate national champion, took place in 1939. It included eight teams.

Not only were the Lakers the NBA's first great team, they also had the first great player. George Mikan was a 6-foot-10 center. He averaged a league-leading 27.4 points per game in the NBA's first season. Only one other player in the league averaged more than 17.8 points per game that year.

"Mikan ran the whole show," said Larry Foust, an All-Star center for the Fort Wayne Pistons from Indiana. "Nobody ever had better offensive moves under the basket."

At the time, most of the great players were power forwards and centers. Bob Pettit, for example, was a 6-foot-9 power forward. He played his entire career for the Hawks. They played in Milwaukee, Wisconsin, and then in St. Louis, Missouri, during Pettit's career. The Hawks have since moved to Atlanta, Georgia. Pettit won the NBA's Most Valuable Player (MVP) Award twice and made the All-Star team in each of his 11 seasons.

## JUMPING JOE

Joe Fulks led the BAA in scoring during its first season in 1946–47 and again in 1947–48. Fulks, who played for the Philadelphia Warriors, is credited with introducing the jump shot to the sport of basketball. The jump shot is when a player releases a shot at the pinnacle of a jump by tossing the ball with their dominant hand and steadying it with the other. It was such an important skill that Fulks has been called the "father of the modern game." Prior to the breakthrough of the jump shot, most players took two-handed set shots. Set shots were attempted with a player's feet still on the ground. They are very rare in modern basketball.

Dolph Schayes, a 6-foot-7 forward/center, played 15 seasons in the NBA with the Syracuse Nationals/Philadelphia 76ers. He made 12 All-Star teams and led his team to the playoffs 14 times.

## Spanning the Globe

The NBA struggled to gain popularity during its early years. Local newspapers barely covered the teams. There was not much coverage on television or radio at that point either.

Part of the reason was because the NBA was not the biggest attraction for basketball fans. The Harlem Globetrotters were actually the most popular team in the country. The Globetrotters were known for their entertainment as much as their skill. Today, the Globetrotters travel the world playing comedy-filled exhibition games. During their early years, however, the Globetrotters played to win. From the start, though, they also entertained crowds with fancy passing and dribbling. Later on, they included comedy in their routines as well.

The Globetrotters formed in Chicago during the 1920s. They helped popularize basketball across the world. But the Globetrotters' greatest moment might have come in 1948. They were playing against Mikan and the Lakers. The Globetrotters won 61–59 on a buzzer-beating shot. The victory proved that the Globetrotters, who were all African Americans, were on equal footing with the Lakers, who were all white. It was also an important moment in the eventual integration of the NBA.

David Stern became NBA commissioner in 1984. He realized the importance of the Globetrotters back in the 1950s. "When you said 'basketball,' people would say 'Harlem Globetrotters,'" he recalled.

**RULE CHANGES**

Because of George Mikan's dominance on both offense and defense, two rules were changed to make the game more fair. First, when Mikan was playing for DePaul University, college basketball outlawed goaltending. That rule kept Mikan from swatting away shots that were either above the rim or on their way down into the basket. Then, once he got to the NBA, the league decided to widen the lane from six to 12 feet (1.83 to 3.66 m) in 1951. Since no player was allowed to stay in the lane for more than three seconds, this rule change limited Mikan's presence around the basket. Big men were often forced to post up farther away from the basket than before.

## Breaking Barriers

Wataru Misaka was technically the first non-white person to play in the NBA. Misaka was a Japanese-American. He played in three games for the New York Knicks during the 1947–48 season, when the league was still known as the BAA.

Three men can claim to be the first African Americans to play in the NBA. Chuck Cooper was the first African-American player to be drafted by an NBA team. The

The **Minneapolis Lakers'** George Mikan, *center*, goes up for a basket between two Harlem Globetrotters players during a 1950 game.

Boston Celtics chose him in the second round of the 1950 NBA Draft. That was three years after Jackie Robinson famously broke Major League Baseball's color barrier.

Nat "Sweetwater" Clifton was the first African-American player to sign a contract with an NBA team. The Knicks signed the former Harlem Globetrotters star in 1950. And Earl Lloyd was the first African American to play in an NBA game when he played for the Washington Capitols in October 1950. Many African Americans would soon become some of the NBA's biggest stars.

# CHAPTER 4

# DYNASTIES AND RIVALRIES

B asketball in the 1960s was dominated by two dynasties. On the college level, it was the University of California, Los Angeles (UCLA) men's basketball team. The UCLA Bruins won the NCAA Tournament 10 times in 12 years between 1964 and 1975. In the NBA, the Boston Celtics dominated, winning 11 championships in 13 years from 1957 to 1969.

## UCLA's Dominance

Led by coach John Wooden, UCLA dominated college basketball unlike any other program in history. The Bruins won 88 straight games between 1970 and 1974. They won 38 straight games in the NCAA Tournament during that period. Under Wooden, UCLA went 149–2 at home between 1965 and 1975.

UCLA basketball coach John Wooden stands with Swen Nater, *left*, and Bill Walton, *right*, in 1972. UCLA won its eighth of 10 NCAA titles in 12 seasons in 1972.

Wooden recruited many great players to UCLA. The two centerpieces were Lew Alcindor (1966 to 1969) and Bill Walton (1971 to 1974). Alcindor, who later changed his name to Kareem Abdul-Jabbar, led the Bruins to three national titles. Walton helped UCLA to two championships. Both men ended up in the Basketball Hall of Fame.

However, the constant at UCLA was Wooden. He coached the Bruins from 1948 to 1975, guiding them to a 620–147 record. He retired after his 10th NCAA championship in 1975.

"Coach Wooden had such an incredible effect on us, not just as basketball players, but as people," Walton said. "He really wasn't even a coach. He was a teacher."

## Boston Rules the NBA

Another legendary coach was at the helm of the Boston Celtics' dynasty. His name was Arnold "Red" Auerbach. He took

### A SHRINE TO BASKETBALL

In 1959, the Naismith Memorial Basketball Hall of Fame was founded in Springfield, Massachusetts. The location was not far from where the sport of basketball had been invented 68 years earlier. The first Hall of Fame class had 17 inductees. Among them were basketball founder Dr. James Naismith, legendary college coach Phog Allen, and the NBA's first superstar, George Mikan.

Bill Russell (6) of the Boston Celtics shoots over the Los Angeles Lakers during a 1969 game.

over the team in 1950 and guided Boston to nine titles before retiring in 1966. Auerbach believed in discipline, teamwork, and most of all, defense.

In 1956, Auerbach found the perfect player for his system— Bill Russell. The Celtics paired Russell, a 6-foot-9 center, with point guard Bob Cousy, and a dynasty was born. Based on his 11 championships in 13 years, Russell is the greatest champion the NBA has ever had. Said Auerbach: "Russell single-handedly revolutionized this game, simply because he made defense so important."

## Wilt the Stilt

The Celtics were the great team of their era, but Russell was not the only great player. In fact, his biggest rival may have been the most dominant player to ever step onto a basketball court.

Wilt Chamberlain was known as "Wilt the Stilt" or "The Big Dipper" because of his stunning size. Chamberlain stood 7-foot-1 in an era when many centers were four or five inches shorter. He entered the NBA in 1959 and quickly began to set records.

Through the end of the 2010–11 season, Chamberlain held more than 70 NBA records. Among them were the highest scoring average for a season (50.4 points per game in 1961–62) and most career rebounds (23,924). His career scoring average (30.07 points per game) is second only to Michael Jordan (30.12).

On March 2, 1962, Chamberlain scored 100 points

### DEFENSIVE STYLES

There are two primary types of defense in basketball: man-to-man defense and zone defense. NBA teams use mostly man-to-man defense, where each of the five players matches up with an opponent and guards that player wherever he goes. Zone defenses were illegal in the NBA until 2001, and NBA teams have been slow to embrace them. In a zone defense, each player is responsible for guarding a specific area of the court. The taller players usually occupy the areas closest to the basket, and the smaller players guard the areas around the free throw and three-point lines.

for the Philadelphia Warriors against the New York Knicks. The performance broke his previous league record of 78 points in one game.

Chamberlain and Russell played 142 games against each other between 1959 and 1969. They met in the playoffs eight times. Russell's Celtics won seven of those series. Still, the battles between Chamberlain and Russell were legendary. "People say it was the greatest individual rivalry they've ever seen," Russell said. "I agree with that."

## The ABA

In 1967, the American Basketball Association (ABA) formed as a competitor to the NBA. It put teams in cities without NBA teams. The ABA also introduced several rules and gimmicks that slightly differed from the NBA. Among them was the three-point line. The NBA adopted the three-point line in 1979–80, and today it is used at all levels of basketball. The ABA also introduced the popular Slam Dunk Contest. The NBA has been doing the same since 1984. The ABA also became known for its red, white, and blue basketball.

The ABA also was the first league to allow teenagers and college underclassmen to play professionally. In 1969, Spencer

Haywood left the University of Detroit after just one season to play for the ABA's Denver Rockets. Five years later, Moses Malone became the first player to jump from high school to the pros when the ABA's Utah Stars drafted him.

The ABA had several great players who played exciting basketball. But the league struggled to match the national attention and following of the more established NBA. So in 1976–77, the leagues merged and four ABA teams joined the NBA. They were the Denver Nuggets, the Indiana Pacers, the New York Nets, and the San Antonio Spurs. The Nets later moved to New Jersey.

The ABA players added an immediate spark to the NBA. In the first season after the merger, Malone was one of ten former ABA players who played in the 1976–77 NBA All-Star Game. Also among that group were future Hall of Famers Rick Barry, George Gervin, and Julius "Dr. J" Erving.

## EXPANSION ERA

The NBA began to take on its current look during the early 1960s. In 1960, the Minneapolis Lakers moved to Los Angeles, California. Two years later, the Philadelphia Warriors moved to San Francisco, California. The Warriors now play in nearby Oakland, California, and are called the Golden State Warriors.

In addition, the league began adding teams in the 1960s. Teams from Chicago, Illinois; San Diego, California; Seattle, Washington; Milwaukee, Wisconsin; and Phoenix, Arizona, joined the NBA between 1961 and 1968. By 1974, the NBA had grown to 18 teams.

The Philadelphia 76ers' Julius Erving rises above his opponents for a dunk during the 1977 NBA All-Star Game.

"At first, the NBA players were very skeptical about us," said Dan Issel, another one of those 1976–77 All-Stars. "We had to prove we belonged, but we did just that."

While the ABA players helped create excitement in the late 1970s, the NBA was still struggling on several levels. Some of the league's superstars were viewed as selfish and unlikable. The league did not have a national television contract. And by 1981, 16 of the 23 teams were losing money. There was talk about folding some of the small-market teams. The league was in a period of financial uncertainty.

## Title IX

A law known as Title IX was put into effect in the United States on June 23, 1972. The law said "a school must provide equal athletic opportunity for both sexes." This included facilities, equipment, supplies, travel, and many other things. It led to a drastic rise in opportunities for women to play sports at colleges and high schools.

The first collegiate women's national championship was held in 1972. An organization called the Association for Intercollegiate Athletics for Women organized women's college basketball through 1982, when the NCAA took control. That, combined with the addition of women's basketball to the Olympic Games in 1976, gave a huge boost to the women's side of the sport. Young stars such as Nancy Lieberman (Old Dominion University) and

### WOMEN'S STARS

There was not an established professional women's basketball league during the 1970s or 1980s. That did not mean there were not some elite players, though. Center Anne Donovan arrived at Old Dominion University in 1979 and played one year with star point guard Nancy Lieberman. The United States did not send a team to the 1980 Olympic Games, but Donovan helped Team USA win gold medals at the 1984 and 1988 Games. Among her teammates in 1984 were University of Southern California forward Cheryl Miller and University of Georgia point guard Teresa Edwards. That was the first of five Olympic Games for Edwards. She finished with four gold medals and one silver medal after the 2000 Games in Sydney, Australia.

Nancy Lieberman, *right,* of Old Dominion takes the ball away from Louisiana Tech's Angela Turner during a 1979 game.

Ann Meyers (UCLA) led Team USA to the 1976 Olympic silver medal. They also starred for their college teams.

The Women's Professional Basketball League formed in 1978 to try to build upon the growing popularity. It was regarded as the first professional basketball league for women. However, it struggled to make money and disbanded in 1981.

In the long run, the progress from Title IX has been huge. There were 400,000 female high school basketball players in 1972. In 1981, there were 4.5 million. Furthermore, only eight states had a high school basketball tournament for girls in 1973. Four years later, 49 of the 50 states had one.

# A BASKETBALL REVOLUTION

At the end of the 1970s, the NBA was in desperate need of a new superstar—or two or three. Fortunately for the league, those stars were about to arrive. And they would change the sport forever.

The main NBA rivalry from the 1980s actually began in the NCAA. The Michigan State Spartans and the Indiana State Sycamores met in the championship game of the 1979 NCAA Tournament. However, most basketball fans viewed the game from an individual perspective: It pitted Earvin "Magic" Johnson against Larry Bird.

Johnson was Michigan State's flashy point guard with a big smile. Bird was Indiana State's power forward with a serious

Larry Bird, *left*, and Magic Johnson pose with the NBA championship trophy in 1984. Their battles for that trophy reignited interest in the NBA.

## MARCH MADNESS

Among the most anticipated sporting events each year are the NCAA Division I basketball tournaments. As of 2011, the top 68 men's teams and 64 women's teams meet in single-elimination postseason tournaments to determine the national champions. The games take place over a three-week period in late March and early April. They are played all over the country and at all times during the day, creating a constant buzz around the event. Many simply refer to the tournaments as March Madness.

Prior to the start of the tournament each year, millions of people fill out a bracket. They attempt to predict the winners of every game, with prizes awaiting those who predict the most winners correctly. In addition to the brackets, the NCAA tournaments are known for their exciting finishes and unlikely upsets. Many consider the 1979 NCAA Tournament that featured Larry Bird and Magic Johnson to be the beginning of today's phenomenon.

demeanor. Both were offensive superstars. And although Johnson was primarily a point guard, he was approximately the same height as Bird—6-foot-9. Johnson's Spartans got the best of Bird's Sycamores, 75–64. But a rivalry was born that night.

Over the next decade, Johnson and Bird would change the face of the NBA. Johnson played for the Los Angeles Lakers. He helped them win five NBA championships between 1980 and 1988. He also was named the league's MVP three times and was a 12-time All-Star.

The Boston Celtics drafted Bird. He led the team to NBA championships in 1981, 1984, and 1986. Like Johnson, Bird also won three MVP Awards and earned 12 All-Star selections. His Celtics and

Johnson's Lakers met three times in the NBA Finals. Los Angeles won two of those series.

"We came along at the right time," Johnson said. "That's all I can say. I needed Larry and he needed me. We pushed each other, meant so much to each other, and meant so much to the game. It was a fun time."

Johnson revolutionized the game by showing the importance of the fast break. His Lakers teams were known as "Showtime" for their fast pace and exciting playmaking. Meanwhile, Bird was the first NBA superstar to take advantage of the three-point line. That was just one of the many areas in which he thrived. Their styles were different, but they were very competitive, particularly with each other.

"The first thing I would do every morning was look at the box scores to see what Magic did," Bird said. "I didn't care about anything else."

## Air Jordan

While Johnson and Bird dominated the 1980s, the 1990s belonged to Michael Jordan. Many people consider the shooting guard for the Chicago Bulls to be the best basketball player ever.

Jordan led the Bulls to six championships between 1991 and 1998. He was named the MVP of the NBA Finals in all six of those series. He also won the league's regular-season MVP Award five times and was a 14-time All-Star. Jordan possibly would have won more titles had he not temporarily retired and missed the 1993–94 season and part of the 1994–95 season.

"In the end, that's all that matters. Winning is why we play the game," Jordan said after winning his sixth NBA title in 1998.

Jordan became known for his spectacular dunks and later on, for his accurate jump shot. Through 2010–11, he holds dozens of NBA records. Among them are most regular-season points per

### STEPPING AWAY

On October 6, 1993, Michael Jordan announced that he was retiring from basketball. The news stunned the sports world. Jordan then announced that he was signing a contract with Major League Baseball's Chicago White Sox. He was planning to play minor league baseball with the hopes of making the major leagues. Jordan played in 127 games in the minors but never made it to the majors. He returned to the Chicago Bulls on March 18, 1995.

The Chicago Bulls' Michael Jordan looks over his shoulder at the Utah Jazz's Bryon Russell during the 1997 NBA Finals.

game (30.12) and most playoff points per game (33.45). "I think he's God disguised as Michael Jordan," Bird once said.

Jordan was the driving force in the global popularity of the NBA. He attracted fans from all over with his exciting plays. He also became a marquee name away from the court. Jordan was a spokesman for many products. Among them were his Air Jordan basketball sneakers, Gatorade, and McDonalds.

Along with Johnson and Bird, Jordan helped bring the NBA to its height of popularity. But as great as all three players were, only one is known as the greatest of all time. As Johnson once said: "There's Michael Jordan. And then there is the rest of us."

## A Boost for Women

Following the passing of Title IX, the 1980s and 1990s became a period of terrific growth in women's basketball. And after the US men's "Dream Team" helped spur international growth with its performance at the 1992 Olympic Games, the 1996 US women's Olympic team made a pretty big impact as well.

The US women had won gold medals at the 1984 and 1988 Olympic Games. But then they settled for a bronze medal at the 1992 Games. Then they again won another bronze medal at the 1994 World Championship. With the 1996 Games at home in Atlanta, Georgia, Team USA set about to reclaim its status as the world's best.

The team had a 10-month international training tour prior to the Games. Behind top players such as center Lisa Leslie and guards Sheryl Swoopes and Teresa Edwards, the team finished

### OH, CANADA

The NBA expanded into Canada in the 1995–96 season. The Toronto Raptors and the Vancouver Grizzlies were added to the league that season. The expansion brought the NBA's total to 29 teams. Due in part to a lack of fan support, the Grizzlies moved to Memphis, Tennessee, in 2001, leaving the Raptors as the only NBA team north of the border.

52–0 on the tour. The games were against other national teams and top US college teams. By the time Team USA reclaimed the gold medal at the 1996 Games, women's basketball was booming in the United States.

After 15 years without a professional women's basketball league, two new leagues formed following the 1996 Games. The American Basketball League folded in 1998, after two seasons. But the Women's National Basketball Association (WNBA) proved stronger. The NBA supported the league financially, helping it overcome the obstacles that had taken down past women's leagues. Although the WNBA was not the first women's professional league, it has become the most successful by far.

The WNBA began with eight teams in the 1997 season. Some of the great players in the WNBA's early years were the same as those who starred on the 1996 US Olympic team. Swoopes, guard Cynthia Cooper, and forward Tina Thompson led the Houston Comets to the first four WNBA titles. Cooper was the MVP of all four WNBA Finals. Leslie then led the Los Angeles Sparks to the next two titles. She earned Finals MVP honors in both wins. New York Liberty center and 1996 Olympian Rebecca Lobo was another early WNBA superstar.

"It's kind of like we were instant superstars," Thompson said. "There was no one before us to make a path."

## The Action Stops

During the 1997–98 season, Minnesota Timberwolves forward Kevin Garnett signed a six-year, $126 million contract. It was the richest deal in the history of professional sports.

NBA owners were growing uncomfortable with the increasing salaries for the players. The owners and the players could not agree on several money-related issues over the next several months. So on July 1, 1998, the owners locked out the players from competing.

The lockout lasted until January 20, 1999. By the time the players and owners came to an agreement, there was only time for a 50-game regular season. Tim Duncan and the San Antonio Spurs won the championship that season. But

### THE HEIGHT OF POPULARITY

Basketball is a sport that people of all heights can play. Most people think of basketball as a sport for tall people. But several shorter players have excelled in the NBA. The shortest of them all was Tyrone "Muggsy" Bogues. He was just 5-foot-3, but he played in the NBA from 1987 to 2001. Anthony "Spud" Webb was just 5-foot-7. Not only did he play in the league from 1985 to 1998, but he also won the Slam Dunk Contest in 1986. And Allen Iverson, who played in the NBA from 1996 to 2010, won an MVP Award and four scoring titles despite only being six feet tall.

Rebecca Lobo, *left*, and Lisa Leslie, *right*, were two of the players from the 1996 US Olympic team who went on to star in the WNBA.

there was an overwhelming feeling that there were no winners that year.

"Everybody lost," said Houston Rockets forward Charles Barkley, a future Hall of Famer. "We lost three months of the season, and we did a disservice to the fans and the game."

# A NEW AGE

As the NBA moved into the new century, a new dynasty appeared. Michael Jordan and the Chicago Bulls had split up after winning their sixth title in the 1998 season. It was time for the Los Angeles Lakers to resume their spot atop the basketball world. Center Shaquille O'Neal and shooting guard Kobe Bryant led the Lakers. Together, the duo led Los Angeles to championships in 2000, 2001, and 2002. O'Neal was one of the most dominant big men the league had seen since George Mikan of the Minneapolis Lakers. Bryant was an athletic playmaker who became one of the league's greatest scorers.

The other great team during the early part of the century was the San Antonio Spurs. They had won the NBA championship during the lockout-shortened 1998–99 season. Two big men

Center Shaquille O'Neal, *left*, and guard Kobe Bryant, *right*, led the Los Angeles Lakers to three straight NBA titles from 2000 to 2002.

nicknamed "The Twin Towers" led San Antonio. Power forward Tim Duncan was 6-foot-11 and center David Robinson was 7-foot-1.

Robinson retired following the 2002–03 season, but Duncan was just getting started. He led the Spurs to two more NBA titles in 2005 and 2007. "No question he's the greatest power forward ever," Robinson said to *USA Today* in 2007. "It's hard to compare anyone to Tim. He's in a class by himself."

## The End of an Era

Following the 2002–03 season, Utah Jazz point guard John Stockton retired. Meanwhile, his longtime teammate with the Jazz, power forward Karl Malone, left to play for the Lakers. Stockton and Malone had played together in Utah since 1985.

The duo became famous for perfecting the "pick and roll." It is a play in which a player sets a screen for the player with the ball. The player then rolls to the basket to accept a pass. Thanks largely to that play, Stockton retired as the NBA's all-time leader in assists. Malone retired in 2004 as the NBA's second all-time leading scorer. They were never quite able to win an NBA title, though. The Jazz reached the NBA Finals in 1997 and 1998 but lost to Jordan and the Bulls there each time.

## New Talent

Prior to 2001, the first pick in the NBA draft had always been a player with US college experience. But that trend changed from 2001 to 2006. Kwame Brown became the first high school player to be taken first overall. The Washington Wizards selected the 19-year-old center in 2001.

High school players would go first overall two more times. In 2003, the Cleveland Cavaliers took local star LeBron James with the first overall pick. He was perhaps the most famous high school

### BAD BEHAVIOR

The NBA endured one of the darkest days in professional sports history on November 19, 2004. The Indiana Pacers were playing a road game against the Detroit Pistons. With less than a minute left, a fight broke out between players on the court. Shortly thereafter, a Pistons fan threw a cup of soda on Pacers forward Ron Artest. Artest then ran into the stands. What began as a brawl between players now included fans as well.

NBA commissioner David Stern called the incident "shocking, repulsive, and inexcusable—a humiliation for everyone associated with the NBA." Artest was suspended for the remainder of the season. Eight other players received suspensions and/or fines as well.

basketball player ever. Some of James's high school games were shown on national television. He even appeared on the cover of a 2002 issue of *Sports Illustrated* under the title "The Chosen One." One year after James went to Cleveland, the Orlando Magic selected teenage center Dwight Howard with the top pick.

The teenage movement was dealt a setback, however. While some teenagers such as James and Howard became stars in the NBA, many more did not. The NBA decided that those players were hurting themselves and the overall quality of the league. So in 2005, the NBA ruled that all incoming players must be at least 19 years old and one year removed from high school.

## College Champs

In the 2000s, several historic college basketball programs returned to the championship level. Coach Mike Krzyzewski had led Duke University to the NCAA title in 1991 and 1992. He then guided the Blue Devils back to two more titles in 2001 and 2010. Many fans enjoy watching Duke basketball teams because they usually play a team-oriented style of basketball. But many people like to root against Duke too. One reason is because Duke's chief rival is another one of the most successful college basketball teams ever.

LeBron James, *right*, poses with NBA commissioner David Stern after the Cleveland Cavaliers selected him with the first pick in the 2003 draft.

The University of North Carolina Tar Heels had won NCAA championships in 1957, 1982, and 1993. A young Michael Jordan made the game-winning shot in the 1982 championship win. Many other stars have played in North Carolina's baby blue uniforms over the years. In 2005 and 2009, new generations of players led the team to two more NCAA titles.

Women's college basketball has not been around as long as men's college basketball. But since 1995, two teams have

Tina Charles lifts teammate Maya Moore after the two led the University of Connecticut to the 2010 NCAA title.

dominated the sport. And two legendary coaches have been at the helm throughout that era.

Coach Geno Auriemma guided the University of Connecticut to seven NCAA championships from 1995 to 2010. Pat Summitt led her Lady Vols from the University of Tennessee to the championship eight times between 1987 and 2008. From 2008 to 2010, Connecticut won 90 consecutive games. That surpassed the previous record of 88 consecutive wins by the UCLA men's team from 1971 to 1974.

Connecticut and Tennessee have sent several players to the WNBA and the Olympic Games. UConn stars such as Sue Bird (2002), Diana Taurasi (2004), Tina Charles (2010), and Maya Moore (2011) were all selected with the first pick in the WNBA Draft. Tennessee players Chamique Holdsclaw (1999) and Candace Parker (2008) also had that honor.

With so many talented players and strong squads, a fierce rivalry developed between the two teams. Even though the top players compete professionally in the WNBA, many consider the Tennessee and UConn rivalry to be the best there is in women's basketball. Author Richard Kent once wrote: "Little girls dream about playing in the UConn-Tennessee game."

## A Lakers-Celtics Revival

In 2008, the Lakers and the Celtics met in the NBA Finals for the eleventh time. It was their first Finals meeting since the 1980s. They had also played for the title in 1984, 1985, and 1987. Many fans were excited for the series between what most consider the NBA's two most iconic teams.

The Celtics defeated the Lakers in the 2008 Finals. However, Los Angeles got its revenge on Boston two years later in their twelfth meeting. As of 2011, the Celtics had the most NBA championships with 17. The Lakers had won 16 titles, although one came in the BAA. The Chicago Bulls were next with six.

## The Big Three

In 2008, James, guard Dwyane Wade, and forward Chris Bosh helped Team USA win a gold medal at the Olympic Games. The three players really enjoyed playing with each other in Beijing, China. And they also could not help but notice that they would all be free agents after the 2010 season.

That off-season, fans were anxiously awaiting where they would sign. When Wade re-signed with the Miami Heat and Bosh joined him there, many people thought James might follow them. They were right. With James, Wade, and Bosh, the Heat instantly became one of the best teams in the NBA. All three players had ranked in the NBA's top 10 in points per game during the 2009–10 season.

Many people rooted for the Heat. However, many others liked rooting against them. Fans were especially mad at James. He left his hometown team, the Cleveland Cavaliers, by making a high-profile announcement during a TV special. But James felt joining Wade and Bosh in Miami would give him his best chance at winning NBA championships.

Despite the Miami Heat's star power, Dirk Nowitzki and the Dallas Mavericks took home their first NBA title in 2011.

The new-look Heat, however, fell short in their first attempt to win an NBA title. In a rematch of the 2006 NBA Finals, the Heat played the Dallas Mavericks. A strong team performance helped the Mavericks defeat the Heat in six games. And in doing so, respected NBA veterans Nowitzki and point guard Jason Kidd won their first titles.

Many fans enjoyed watching the 2011 NBA Finals. The series showcased hard work, exciting action, and lots of teamwork. Those same qualities have been entertaining basketball fans and players for more than a century.

| 1891 | Dr. James Naismith, a physical education instructor in Springfield, Massachusetts, invents the sport of basketball. The first players are his students, who play a game with nine players on each side. |
| 1895 | The first game between two colleges takes place at Hamline University in St. Paul, Minnesota. The winner is the Minnesota School of Agriculture, which defeats Hamline 9–3. |
| 1899 | Senda Berenson publishes the "Official Rules" of women's basketball. Berenson is the director of physical education at Smith College in Northampton, Massachusetts. |
| 1905 | Representatives from 15 colleges meet in Philadelphia, Pennsylvania, and form the Basket Ball Rules Committee. This organization eventually becomes the NCAA. |
| 1936 | Basketball is added to the Olympic Games. Naismith is invited to toss the ceremonial ball for the first Olympic game in Berlin, Germany. |
| 1946 | The BAA is formed. Three years later, the league merges with the NBL to form the NBA. |
| 1949 | Led by superstar center George Mikan, the Minneapolis Lakers win the first NBA championship. They defeat the Syracuse Nationals in six games. |
| 1950 | The NBA color barrier is broken. Chuck Cooper is the first African-American player to be drafted by an NBA team, while Nat "Sweetwater" Clifton is the first African-American player to sign a contract with an NBA team, and Earl Lloyd is the first African-American to play in an NBA game. |
| 1957 | The Boston Celtics win the NBA championship. The title begins a stretch of 11 championships in 13 years with center Bill Russell leading the way. |

| 1962 | Wilt Chamberlain of the Philadelphia Warriors scores 100 points in a game against the New York Knicks. The performance, which takes place in Hershey, Pennsylvania, breaks Chamberlain's previous NBA record of 78 points. |

| 1964 | UCLA wins the NCAA championship. The title begins a stretch of 10 championships in 12 years under coach John Wooden. It remains unmatched in men's and women's college basketball. |

| 1972 | A law known as Title IX is put into effect in the United States. The law gives women an equal opportunity to play sports at schools and changes women's athletics forever. |

| 1976 | The ABA merges with the NBA. Four ABA teams are absorbed into the NBA, bringing the NBA's total to 22 teams. |

| 1984 | Larry Bird and Earvin "Magic" Johnson meet in the NBA Finals for the first of three times. Bird's Celtics defeat Johnson's Los Angeles Lakers in seven games. |

| 1992 | The US Olympic team, known as the Dream Team, wins the gold medal in Barcelona, Spain. It is the first Olympic Games in which professional players are allowed to participate for the United States. |

| 1997 | The WNBA plays its first season. The Houston Comets win the first four WNBA championships. |

| 1998 | Michael Jordan wins his sixth and final NBA championship with the Chicago Bulls. Jordan wins the title by making a jump shot with 5.2 seconds left in Game 6 against the Utah Jazz. |

| 2010 | The Miami Heat sign free agents LeBron James, Dwyane Wade, and Chris Bosh. The three players had been drafted in the same class in 2003 and helped Team USA win Olympic gold in 2008. However, the Dallas Mavericks defeat the Heat in the 2011 NBA Finals. |

## MEN

**Kareem Abdul-Jabbar**
center

**Larry Bird**
forward

**Kobe Bryant**
guard

**Wilt Chamberlain**
center

**Tim Duncan**
forward

**Julius "Dr. J." Erving**
forward

**John Havlicek**
guard

**Earvin "Magic" Johnson**
guard

**Michael Jordan**
guard

**Karl Malone**
forward

**George Mikan**
center

**Hakeem Olajuwon**
center

**Shaquille O'Neal**
center

**Oscar Robertson**
guard

**Bill Russell**
center

**John Stockton**
guard

**Bill Walton**
center

**Jerry West**
guard

## WOMEN

**Cynthia Cooper**
guard

**Babe Didrikson**
forward

**Anne Donovan**
center

**Teresa Edwards**
guard

**Lisa Leslie**
center

**Nancy Lieberman**
guard

**Ann Meyers**
guard

**Cheryl Miller**
forward

**Sheryl Swoopes**
forward

**All-American**

A group of players chosen as the best in the country in a particular activity.

**assist**

A pass that directly leads to a teammate's made basket.

**barnstormers**

Players who tour an area playing exhibition games.

**commissioner**

An official selected by an athletic association or league to exercise administrative powers.

**draft**

The system of selecting amateur players by professional teams.

**dunk**

To throw the ball into the basket with a forceful motion.

**dynasty**

A team that dominates a sport or league for multiple years.

**free agent**

A professional athlete who is allowed to sign a contract with any team.

**integration**

When players of different racial groups are let into something, such as the NBA.

**lockout**

The withholding of employment by an employer and the closing of a business. NBA owners can lock out the players if the sides disagree over labor issues.

**rebound**

The gathering of a missed shot after it hits the rim or the backboard.

**recruit**

To attempt to secure the services of a player.

**referee**

An official who supervises the play in a game.

**rival**

A person or team that competes with another person or team for a similar goal.

**tip-off**

A jump ball at the start of a basketball game.

## Selected Bibliography

Ballard, Chris. *The Art of a Beautiful Game*. New York: Simon and Schuster, 2009. Print.

Cherry, Robert. *Wilt: Larger than Life*. Chicago: Triumph Books, 2004. Print.

Fox, Larry. *The Illustrated History of Basketball*. New York: Grosset & Dunlap, 1974. Print.

*Hoops Heaven*. Overland Park, KS: Ascend Books, 2009. Print.

Pluto, Terry. *Loose Balls*. New York: Fireside, 1990. Print.

*Sport in America*. Champaign, IL: Human Kinetics, 2010. Print.

Wright, Frank L. *The Ultimate Basketball Book*. Crystal Bay, NV: Sierra Vista Publications, 2007. Print.

## Further Readings

*The Macrophenomenal Pro Basketball Almanac*. New York: FreeDarko High Council, 2008. Print.

*The Undisputed Guide to Pro Basketball History*. New York: FreeDarko High Council, 2010. Print.

*Total Basketball: The Ultimate Basketball Encyclopedia*. Wilmington, DE: Sport Media Publishing, 2003. Print.

## Web Links

To learn more about basketball, visit ABDO Publishing Company online at **www.abdopublishing.com**. Web sites about basketball are featured on our Book Links page. These links are routinely monitored and updated to provide the most current information available.

## Places to Visit

### College Basketball Experience

1401 Grand Boulevard
Kansas City, MO 64106
(816) 949-7500
www.collegebasketballexperience.com
This interactive museum allows visitors to experience various aspects of college basketball. It also includes the National Collegiate Basketball Hall of Fame, which highlights the greatest players, coaches, and moments in the history of college basketball.

### Naismith Memorial Basketball Hall of Fame

1000 West Columbus Avenue
Springfield, MA 01105
(413) 781-6500
www.hoophall.com
This hall of fame and museum highlights the greatest players and moments in the history of basketball. Among the people enshrined here are Michael Jordan, Nancy Lieberman, George Mikan, and basketball's inventor himself, James Naismith.

## About the Author

Drew Silverman is a sportswriter based in Philadelphia, Pennsylvania. He graduated from Syracuse University in 2004. He then worked as a sportswriter and editor at ESPN's headquarters in Bristol, Connecticut, before returning back home to Philly. After several years as the sports editor for *The Bulletin* newspaper, he began working for Comcast SportsNet as a content manager.